Meet Emilie Richards

Photo by Creation Waits

*N*ow a USA TODAY bestselling author of women's fiction, Emilie Richards recalls fondly the months she served as a VISTA volunteer in the Arkansas Ozarks.

"This was the country's third poorest county," Emilie said in an interview from her Virginia home. "They had no phones, no safe water supply and no indoor plumbing. But the women created beauty out of nothing – turning scraps of old clothing and feedsacks into exquisitely beautiful quilts."

Emilie said the women insisted she quilt with them in the evenings, "and then later, they'd take out my stitches," she laughingly recalls of her early attempts at the craft.

The 20-year-old college student was left with a richness of experience and a love of quilting that would forever change her life and ultimately inspire a series of novels about the age-old craft. Emilie went on to finish her undergraduate degree in American studies and her master's in family development. She served as a therapist in a mental health center, as a parent services coordinator for Head Start families and in several pastoral counseling centers. Now a full-time writer, Emilie has drawn on these experiences while crafting more than 50 novels.

In *Wedding Ring*, the first Shenandoah Album novel, Emilie uses the stages of quilting as a metaphor for the cycles of marriage. In *Endless Chain*, Emilie's July 2005 hardcover novel, quilting serves as an activity that binds a community together in two parallel stories about human rights. Two pattern books, *Quilt Along with Emilie Richards — Wedding Ring* and *Endless Chain*, offer Emilie's fans a chance to create their own versions of the quilts in her novels.

And Emilie has just been named the first member of ABC Quilts' National Advisory Board. The non-profit group, headquartered in Northwood, N.H., teaches people of all ages to quilt and works to prevent HIV/AIDS and alcohol and drug abuse. The group's international network of volunteers has delivered over a half million quilts since they were founded in 1988.

To learn more about Emilie Richards and ABC Quilts, visit Emilie's Web site at www.emilierichards.com.

LEISURE ARTS, INC.
Little Rock, Arkansas

Read the Books That *Inspired* the Projects

Leisure Arts is pleased to offer these two quilting instruction books as companions to Emilie's compelling stories.

Quilt Along with Emilie Richards: Wedding Ring includes complete instructions for creating eight quilts from the story … Wedding Ring, Friendship Album, North Carolina Lily, Tree of Life, Cissy's Pinwheel, Helen's Star, Simple Pleasures, and Sunbonnet Sue.

And if you would like to make Elisa's throw-sized Endless Chain Quilt, then you won't want to miss the second instruction book, *Quilt Along with Emilie Richards: Endless Chain*. This collection of six quilt patterns also includes Chinese Coins, Autumn Leaves, La Casa Amarilla, Clay's Choice, and Patriotic Sampler.

Enhanced with excerpts from the novels, each quilting instruction book gives the reader a glimpse of the fascinating characters created by the gifted author.

The first two novels in Emilie Richards' *Shenandoah Album* series, *Wedding Ring* and *Endless Chain*, are rich with family drama, romance — and quilts!

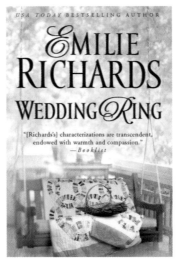 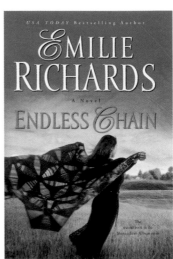

Read Emilie Richards' **Shenandoah Album** novels, then quilt along with the women of Toms Brook and Fitch Crossing Road. You may just discover a lifelong passion of your very own!

2

Meet the Women from Wedding Ring

Tessa MacCrae

Tessa MacCrae feels as if she's facing a prison sentence when she reluctantly agrees to spend the summer helping her mother and grandmother clean out and repair the old family home in Virginia's Shenandoah Valley. She is prepared for inevitable anger and tension — the only emotional bonds they've ever shared. The three women have never been close, but Tessa hopes that time away from her husband — no matter how trying — will help her find the answers she desperately seeks and come to a decision about her failing marriage.

Nancy Whitlock

Nancy, Tessa's mother, appears to be little more than a hand-wringing social climber, who spends her days entertaining and courting Richmond's wealthy elite. What Tessa can't see is the woman so ashamed of her roots and desperate for acceptance that she would do anything to be loved, or the anxious wife trying to hold on to a marriage on which she has never had a firm grasp.

"When I was a little girl, Mama would wash her quilts twice a year. She'd wash them in an old tub outside before she hung them on the line. I loved them that way. Waving in the breeze, like dancing rainbows."
— *Nancy Whitlock,*
Wedding Ring

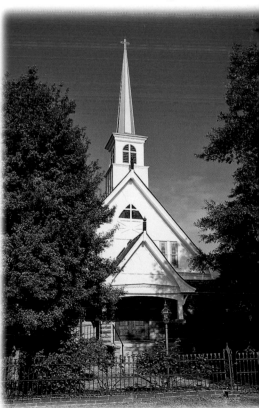

3

"Wedding ring," Tessa said to Nancy. "I remember now. You told me that's what it was called. It was made from dozens of fabrics. I slept under it as a child. I loved it. I always slept better when you let me have it on my bed."

— from Wedding Ring

"That's the thing about quilts. They're art you can feel all around you. Not that many paintings you can hug this way."
— *Nancy Whitlock,*
Wedding Ring

Helen Henry

Helen, the family matriarch, is domineering, sharp-tongued and incapable of sharing feelings — except negative ones. Widowed at a young age, she has struggled her whole life, hanging on to the family farm by sacrificing everything, particularly love. Fiercely independent, Helen resents her daughter and granddaughter's intrusion, too angry to admit that she needs their help.

Cissy Mowrey

Being a teenager isn't easy, but Cissy Mowrey never complains. Worrying other people with her problems just isn't a part of her nature, not even when she's possessed of a keen desire to learn how to quilt for her unborn child. Despite their reservations about Cissy's unmarried state, Helen and Tessa find themselves drawn to their young neighbor's sunny nature, and the quilting lessons begin … even though the older women already have enough problems of their own.

But with the passing weeks, each of the women's lives begins to change. Here in her grandmother's house, Tessa comes face-to-face with the family and the history that has shaped her. As Tessa restores a tattered wedding-ring quilt pieced by her grandmother and quilted by her mother years ago, the secrets that have shadowed their lives unfold in a drama of discovery, hope and healing. For the first time, Tessa can look past the years of resentment and regret and see her mother and grandmother for the flawed but courageous women they are. Through days of hard work, simple living and the determination to repair the torn fabric of their own lives, Tessa, Nancy, and Helen will discover that what was lost can be found again — if they look deeply into their hearts.

"If you do something that makes the world a beautiful place, you're supposed to show it to people. God gave you that talent. And now you have to give it back in the form of pleasure to the eyes."
— *Cissy Mowrey,*
Wedding Ring

Double Wedding Ring

The Wedding Ring quilt that Helen pieced held a wealth of meaning for her family. No two scrap quilts are ever alike, and our quilt doesn't have a blue background like Helen's. However, feel free to substitute blue fabric for some or all of the white background pieces. Whatever fabrics you choose, your quilt is sure to be an original … just like Helen's.

QUILT SIZE: 67³/₈" x 81³/₈" (171 cm x 207 cm)
FINISHED BLOCK SIZE: 10" diameter (25 cm)

Note: While our version of the Double Wedding Ring quilt is not an exact match to the quilt shown on the cover, it will look equally lovely in your home.

CUTTING OUT THE PIECES

Refer to **Rotary Cutting***, page 50, to cut strips. All measurements include a ¹/₄" seam allowance. Refer to* **Template Cutting***, page 50, to use patterns, page 11.*

From assorted prints:
- Cut 1744 (**A's**) from template.
- Cut 436 (**B's**) from template.
- Cut 436 (**B's reversed**) from template.

From cream solid:
- Cut 218 (**C's**) from template.
- Cut 99 (**D's**) from template.

From pink solid:
- Cut 9 strips 1⁵/₈"w. From these strips, cut 216 **squares** (**E**) 1⁵/₈" x 1⁵/₈".

From green solid:
- Cut 10 strips 1⁵/₈"w. From these strips, cut 220 **squares** (**F**) 1⁵/₈" x 1⁵/₈".

YARDAGE REQUIREMENTS

Yardage is based on 43"/44" (109 cm/112 cm) wide fabric.

9 yds (8.2 m) **total** of assorted print fabrics

6¹/₂ yds (5.9 m) of cream solid fabric

¹/₂ yd (46 cm) of pink solid fabric

¹/₂ yd (46 cm) of green solid fabric

5 yds (4.6 m) of backing fabric

⁷/₈ yd (80 cm) of binding fabric

You will also need:
76" x 90" (193 cm x 229 cm) rectangle of batting

Template plastic

Permanent fine-point pen

Unit 1 (make 436)

Unit 2 (make 108)

Unit 3 (make 110)

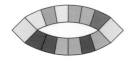

Unit 4 (make 218)

Unit 5 (make 108)

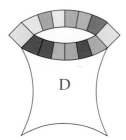

Unit 6 (make 110)

Wedding Ring Block Diagram (make 50)

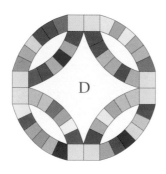

Top/Bottom Setting Block (make 8)

Side Setting Block (make 10)

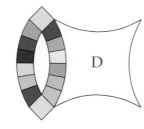

ASSEMBLING THE QUILT TOP

*Follow **Piecing and Pressing**, page 51, to assemble the quilt top.*

1. Sew 1 (B), 4 (A's) and 1 (B reversed) together to make **Unit 1**. Make 436 **Unit 1's**.

2. Sew 1 pink **square** (E) to each end of a **Unit 1** to make **Unit 2**. Make 108 **Unit 2's**.

3. Sew 1 green **square** (F) to each end of a **Unit 1** to make **Unit 3**. Make 110 **Unit 3's**.

*Note: For curved seams in **Steps 4 — 8**, match centers and pin at center and at dots, then match and pin between these points. Sew seams with cream background pieces (C or D) on top, easing in fullness from pieced units.*

4. Sew 1 **Unit 1** and 1 (C) together to make **Unit 4**. Make 218 **Unit 4's**.

5. Sew 1 **Unit 2** and 1 **Unit 4** together to make **Unit 5**. Make 108 **Unit 5's**.

6. Sew 1 **Unit 3** and 1 **Unit 4** together to make **Unit 6**. Make 110 **Unit 6's**.

7. Referring to **Wedding Ring Block Diagram**, sew 2 **Unit 5's**, 2 **Unit 6's** and 1 (D) together to make **Wedding Ring Block**. Make 50 **Blocks**.

8. Referring to **Setting Block Diagrams**, sew 1 **Unit 5** and 1 (D) together to make **Top/Bottom Setting Block**. Make 8 **Top/Bottom Setting Blocks**. Sew 1 **Unit 6** and 1 (D) together to make **Side Setting Block**. Make 10 **Side Setting Blocks**.

9. Referring to **Assembly Diagram**, sew **Wedding Ring Blocks**, **Setting Blocks** and remaining **D's** together into horizontal **Rows**. Sew **Rows** together to complete **Quilt Top**.

COMPLETING THE QUILT

1. Follow **Quilting**, page 54, to mark, layer, and quilt as desired. Our quilt is hand quilted in the ditch around the rings. There is an "X" quilted in the center of each ring.

2. To prepare quilt for binding, straight stitch around quilt $^1/_8$" from raw edge. Trim backing and batting even with raw edge of quilt top.

3. Cut a 29" square of binding fabric. Follow **Making Continuous Bias Binding**, page 59, to make approximately 10 yards of 2"w bias binding.

4. Follow **Attaching Binding with Mitered Corners**, page 60, **Steps 1 — 2** to pin binding to front of quilt, easing binding around curved edges. Sew binding to quilt until binding overlaps beginning end by approximately 2". Trim excess binding. Fold binding over to quilt backing and pin in place, covering stitching line. Blindstitch binding to backing.

Assembly Diagram

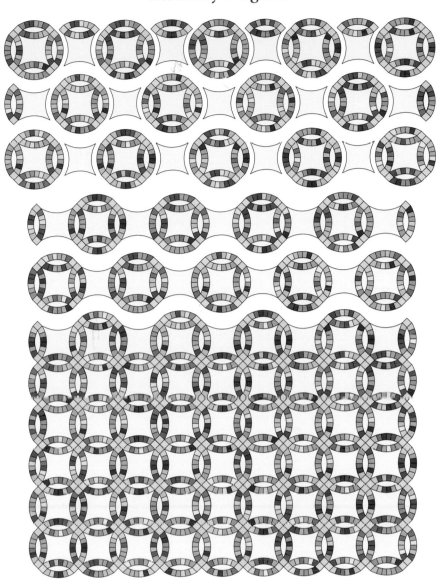

9

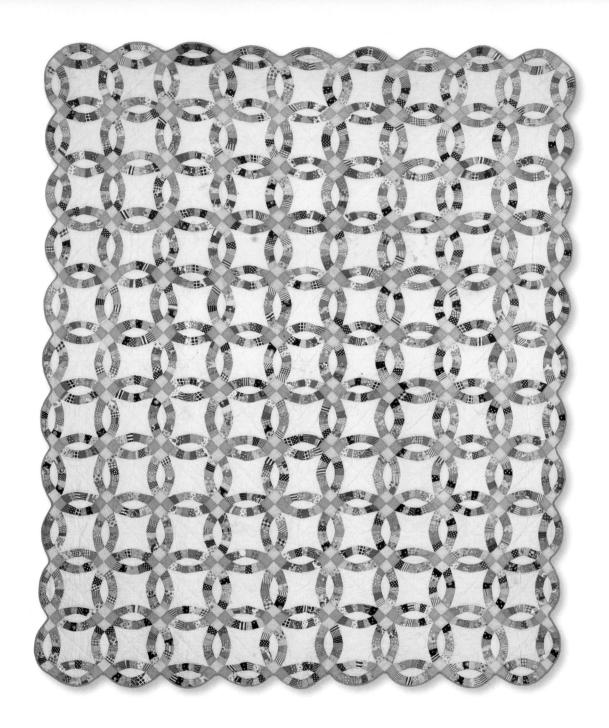

"*The final layer in the trunk, under a neatly folded white sheet, was the wedding ring quilt. Tessa lifted it carefully, excitement mounting as she pulled it from the trunk. The past seemed to be impregnated in the cloth. Tessa was filled with memories from her childhood.*"
— from Wedding Ring

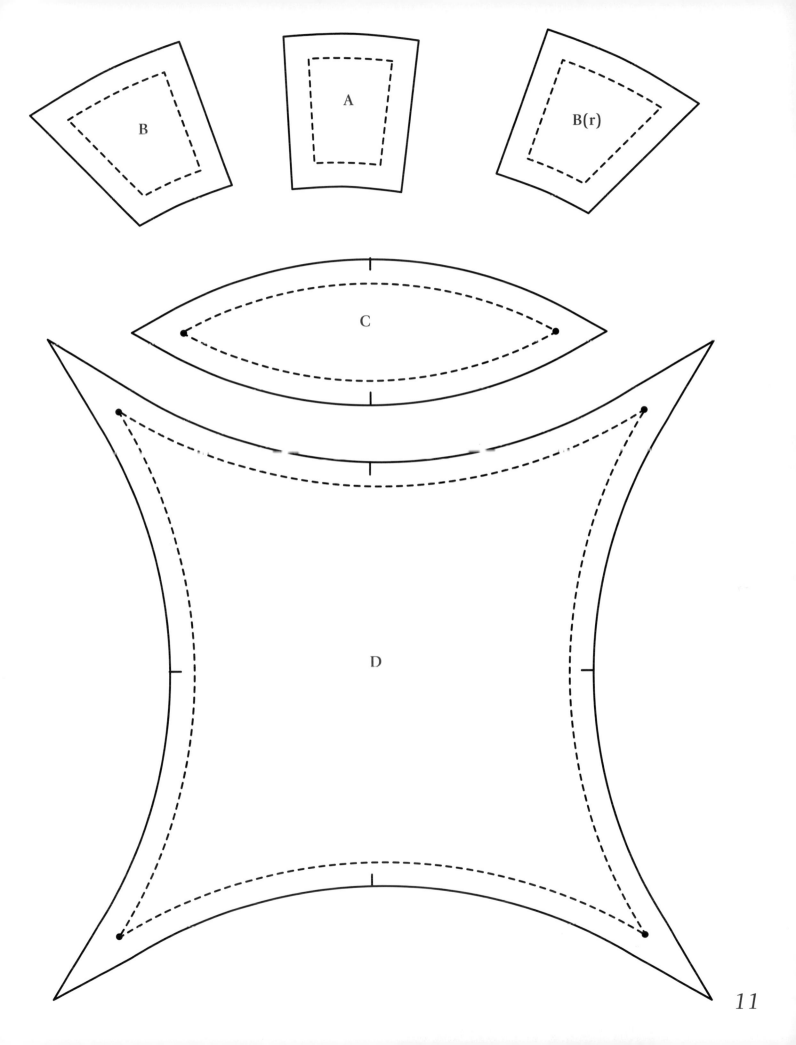

B

A

B(r)

C

D

11

Friendship Album

When Helen was a little girl, she desperately wished to take part in the quilting bee to help make a Friendship Album quilt for her teacher. Instead, she was assigned babysitting duty, a chore that held no interest for her. The quilt we found may be very much like the ones made in the Shenandoah Valley region in the early 1900's. But the pale centers of its blocks are still awaiting signatures, so we can assume it was not made as a gift, but by an individual who simply admired the design and wanted to use it in her own household.

QUILT SIZE: 73½" x 90½" (187 cm x 230 cm)
FINISHED BLOCK SIZE: 12½" x 12½" (32 cm x 32 cm)

12

YARDAGE REQUIREMENTS
Yardage is based on 43"/44" (109 cm/112 cm) wide fabric.

2⅝ yds (2.4 m) of blue print fabric

⅝ yd (57 cm) of blue check fabric

⅛ yd (11 cm) **each** of 20 light print fabrics

⅛ yd (11 cm) **each** of 20 dark print fabrics

5½ yds (5 m) of backing fabric

⅞ yd (80 cm) of binding fabric

You will also need: 82" x 98" (208 cm x 249 cm) rectangle of batting

CUTTING OUT THE PIECES

*Follow **Rotary Cutting**, page 50, to cut fabric. All measurements include a ¹/₄" seam allowance.*

From blue print:
- Cut 17 strips 5"w. From these strips, cut 49 **sashing strips (A)** 5" x 13".

From blue check:
- Cut 4 strips 5"w. From these strips, cut 30 **sashing squares (B)** 5" x 5".

From *each* light print:
- Cut 1 strip 3"w. From this strip, cut 10 **squares (C)** 3" x 3".
- Cut 1 **rectangle (D)** 3" x 8".

From *each* dark print:
- Cut 1 strip 3"w. From this strip, cut 12 **squares (E)** 3" x 3".

13

Block (make 20)

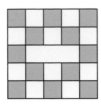

Block (make 20)

Row (make 5)

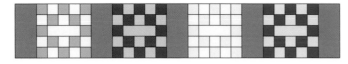

Sashing Row (make 6)

ASSEMBLING THE QUILT TOP

Follow Piecing and Pressing, page 51, to assemble the quilt top.

1. Referring to **Block Diagram**, sew 1 **rectangle** (**D**), 10 **squares** (**C**), and 12 **squares** (**E**) together to make **Block**. Make 20 **Blocks**.

2. Referring to **Row Diagram**, sew 4 **Blocks** and 5 **sashing strips** (**A**) together to make **Row**. Make 5 **Rows**.

3. Referring to **Sashing Row Diagram**, sew 5 **sashing squares** (**B**) and 4 **sashing strips** (**A**) together to make **Sashing Row**. Make 6 **Sashing Rows**.

4. Sew **Rows** and **Sashing Rows** together to complete **Quilt Top**.

COMPLETING THE QUILT TOP

1. Follow **Quilting**, page 54, to mark, layer, and quilt as desired. Our quilt is machine quilted with a flower in the blocks, an "X" in the sashing squares, and parallel lines in the sashings.

2. Cut a 30" square of binding fabric. Follow **Binding**, page 59, to bind quilt using $2^1/_2$"w bias binding with mitered corners.

"*Tessa stood in the doorway of the sanctuary and watched her grandmother and a curator from the Virginia Quilt Museum discussing each quilt. Helen still looked shell-shocked. After today, she would never be able to think of herself as a simple country quilter again. The woman from the museum was using terms like* luminosity, emotional resonance *and* dramatic focus. *Helen was simply nodding.*"

— from Wedding Ring

15

North Carolina Lily

Helen loves classic quilt patterns, but to Nancy and Tessa's surprise, Helen doesn't always create her quilts in the expected colors. Her latest North Carolina Lily quilt sparkles in jewel-tone hues, a break with tradition that her family found delightful.

QUILT SIZE: 44" x 44" (112 cm x 112 cm)
FINISHED BLOCK SIZE: 12" x 12" (30 cm x 30 cm)

CUTTING OUT THE PIECES

*Refer to **Rotary Cutting**, page 50, to cut strips. All measurements include a $^1/_4$" seam allowance. Refer to **Template Cutting**, page 50, to use pattern, page 20. Cutting lengths given for borders are exact.*

From black solid:
- Cut 1 strip $3^1/_4$"w. From this strip, cut 8 squares $3^1/_4$" x $3^1/_4$". Cut each square in half twice diagonally to make 32 **triangles (A)**.
- Cut 1 strip $2^1/_2$"w. From this strip, cut 16 **squares (B)** $2^1/_2$" x $2^1/_2$".
- Cut 1 strip $4^1/_2$"w. From this strip, cut 8 **squares (C)** $4^1/_2$" x $4^1/_2$".
- Cut 1 strip $8^1/_2$"w. From this strip, cut 4 **squares (D)** $8^1/_2$" x $8^1/_2$".
- Cut 1 **setting square (E)** $12^1/_2$" x $12^1/_2$".
- Cut 2 squares $9^3/_8$" x $9^3/_8$". Cut each square in half once diagonally to make 4 **corner triangles (F)**.
- Cut 1 square $18^1/_4$" x $18^1/_4$". Cut square in half twice diagonally to make 4 **setting triangles (G)**.
- Cut 4 **outer borders (H)** $4^1/_2$" x $35^1/_2$".
- Cut 1 **binding square** 23" x 23".

From pink print No. 1:
- Cut 1 square $4^7/_8$" x $4^7/_8$". Cut square in half once diagonally to make 2 **triangles (I)**.
- Cut 1 square $3^1/_4$" x $3^1/_4$". Cut square in half twice diagonally to make 4 **triangles (J)**.

From pink print No. 2:
- Cut 2 squares $4^7/_8$" x $4^7/_8$". Cut each square in half once diagonally to make 4 **triangles (I)**. You will use 3 **I's**.
- Cut 2 squares $3^1/_4$" x $3^1/_4$". Cut each square in half twice diagonally to make 8 **triangles (J)**. You will use 6 **J's**.

From pink print No. 3:
- Cut 2 squares $4^7/_8$" x $4^7/_8$". Cut each square in half once diagonally to make 4 **triangles (I)**. You will use 3 **I's**.
- Cut 2 squares $3^1/_4$" x $3^1/_4$". Cut each square in half twice diagonally to make 8 **triangles (J)**. You will use 6 **J's**.

From purple print No. 1:
- Cut 1 square $4^7/_8$" x $4^7/_8$". Cut square in half once diagonally to make 2 **triangles (I)**.
- Cut 1 square $3^1/_4$" x $3^1/_4$". Cut square in half twice diagonally to make 4 **triangles (J)**.

From purple print No. 2:
- Cut 2 squares $4^7/_8$" x $4^7/_8$". Cut each square in half once diagonally to make 4 **triangles (I)**. You will use 3 **I's**.
- Cut 2 squares $3^1/_4$" x $3^1/_4$". Cut each square in half twice diagonally to make 8 **triangles (J)**. You will use 6 **J's**.

YARDAGE REQUIREMENTS
Yardage is based on 43"/44" (109 cm/112 cm) wide fabric.

$2^7/_8$ yds (2.6 m) of black solid fabric (includes binding)

$^1/_4$ yd (23 cm) **each** of 3 pink print and 3 purple print fabrics

$^3/_8$ yd (34 cm) of teal print fabric

3 yds (2.7 m) of backing fabric

You will also need:
52" x 52" (132 cm x 132 cm) rectangle of batting

Template plastic

Permanent fine-point pen

Applique Block (make 4)

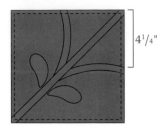

4¹/₄"

Unit 1 (make 2)

Unit 2 (make 2)

Unit 3 (make 2)

Flower (make 2)

Unit 4

Unit 5

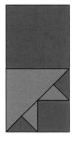

18

From purple print No. 3:
- Cut 2 squares 4⁷/₈" x 4⁷/₈". Cut each square in half once diagonally to make 4 **triangles (I)**. You will use 3 **I's**.
- Cut 2 squares 3¹/₄" x 3¹/₄". Cut each square in half twice diagonally to make 8 **triangles (J)**. You will use 6 **J's**.

From teal print:
- Cut 2 **side inner borders (K)** 1" x 34¹/₂".
- Cut 2 **top/bottom inner borders (L)** 1" x 35¹/₂".
- Cut 4 **squares (M)** 2¹/₂" x 2¹/₂".
- Cut 4 **leaves (N)**. Cut 4 leaves in reverse (**Nr**).
- Cut 4 **bias center stems (O)** 1" x 12¹/₂".
- Cut 8 **bias left and right stems (P)** 1" x 6¹/₂".

MAKING THE BLOCKS

*Follow **Piecing and Pressing**, page 51, to assemble the quilt top. Refer to **Needle-Turn Appliqué**, page 52, for appliqué technique.*

1. Fold square (**D**) in half; finger press fold. Fold square in half again and finger press folds. Referring to **Appliqué Block**, appliqué 2 stems (**P**) 1 stem (**O**), 1 leaf (**N**), and 1 leaf (**Nr**) in reverse on 1 square (**D**). Make 4 **Appliqué Blocks**.

2. Sew 1 purple print #1 **triangle (J)** to 1 black **triangle (A)** to make **Unit 1** and **Unit 2**. Make 2 **Unit 1's** and 2 **Unit 2's**.

3. Sew 1 **Unit 1** and 1 **Unit 2** to adjacent sides of 1 **square (B)** to make **Unit 3**. Make 2 **Unit 3's**.

4. Sew 1 **Unit 3** to 1 purple print #1 **triangle (I)** to make **Flower**. Make 2 purple print #1 **Flowers**.

5. Repeat **Steps 2 — 4** to make 3 purple print #2 **Flowers**, 3 purple print #3 **Flowers**, 2 pink print #1 **Flowers**, 3 pink print #2 **Flowers**, and 3 pink print #3 **Flowers**.

    (**Note:** Referring to **Assembly Diagram**, page 20, for Flower placement, follow **Steps 6 — 10** to make 4 Blocks).

6. Sew 2 **Flowers** and 1 **square (C)** together to make **Unit 4**.

7. Sew 1 **Flower** and 1 **square (C)** together to make **Unit 5**.

8. Sew **Unit 5** to **Appliqué Block** to make **Unit 6**.

9. Sew **Unit 4** to **Unit 6** to make **Unit 7**.

10. Draw a diagonal line (corner to corner) on wrong side of 1 **square** (M). Place square on corner of **Unit 7** over end of stem. Stitch on drawn line (**Fig. 1**). Trim $1/4$" from stitching line. Open and press, pressing seam allowance to darker fabric to complete **Block**.

"$\mathcal{N}$ancy spread open Helen's most recent North Carolina Lily quilt. Helen had probably made half a dozen of that pattern over her lifetime, most in the traditional reds and greens on a white background. This time, though, she'd followed her own heart and made the lilies of bolder shades of pinks, purples and teal, and set them on black."

— from Wedding Ring

Unit 6

Unit 7

Fig. 1

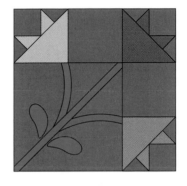

Block

19

ASSEMBLING THE QUILT TOP

Refer to Assembly Diagram for placement.

1. Sew 1 **Block**, 2 **setting triangles** (G), and 1 **corner triangle** (F) together to make **Row 1**.

2. Sew 2 **Blocks**, **setting square** (E), and 2 **corner triangles** (F) together to make **Row 2**.

3. Sew 1 **Block**, 2 **setting triangles** (G), and 1 **corner triangle** (F) together to make **Row 3**.

4. Sew **Rows 1 — 3** together to complete **Wall Hanging Top Center**.

5. Sew **side inner borders** (K), then **top** and **bottom inner borders** (L) to wall hanging top center.

6. Sew **side outer borders** (H) to wall hanging top center.

7. Sew 1 **Flower** to each end of **top** and **bottom outer borders** (H). Sew top and bottom outer borders to wall hanging top.

Assembly Diagram

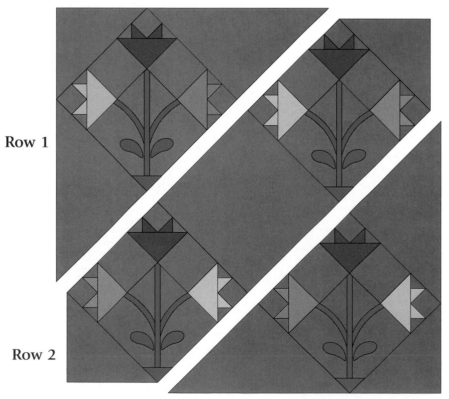

Row 1

Row 2

Row 3

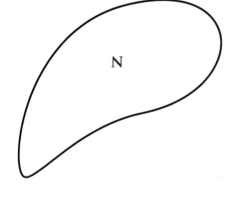

N

20

COMPLETING THE QUILT

1. Follow **Quilting**, page 54, to mark, layer and quilt as desired. We used variegated thread to machine quilt a feathered wreath in the setting square and a feathered design in the setting triangles, corner triangles, and borders. We used black thread to outline quilt around each flower and to quilt around each feathered design in the borders. Then to give the quilt depth, we added closely stitched free-motion quilting in the remaining black background areas.

2. Follow **Making Continuous Bias Binding**, page 59, and use **binding square** to make $2^1/2$"w bias binding.

3. Follow **Attaching Binding with Mitered Corners**, page 60, to attach binding.

"Helen had always worked on more than one project at a time. It was a luxury of sorts not to finish one quilt before starting another, one of the few things she did simply because it felt good. Pleasing herself that way felt almost sinful, but there it was. She was going to keep on doing it."

— from Wedding Ring

Tree of Life

A Tree of Life quilt can be either a simple patchwork construction or an elaborate work of appliqué. Both styles were inspired by the biblical tree of life that grew in the Garden of Eden. Helen's version of the quilt is a classic red-on-white design of pieced blocks.

QUILT SIZE: 76" x 76" (193 cm x 193 cm)
FINISHED BLOCK SIZE: 12$\frac{1}{2}$" x 12$\frac{1}{2}$" (32 cm x 32 cm)

CUTTING OUT THE PIECES

*Refer to **Template Cutting**, page 50, to use pattern, page 27. Refer to **Rotary Cutting**, page 50, to cut strips. All measurements include a ¹/₄" seam allowance.*

*(**Note:** A large number of Triangle-Squares are needed for this project. To make piecing faster and to help with accurate sewing of the Triangle-Squares, you might choose to use a product for making Triangle-Squares such as Triangles On A Roll or Thangles™. You buy these according to the finished size of the Triangle-Square. These are 1¹/₄" finished Triangle-Squares.)*

From white solid:
- Cut 36 (**A's**) from template; cut 36 (**A's**) in reverse from template.
- Cut 9 strips 5⁷/₈"w. From these strips, cut 54 **squares** 5⁷/₈" x 5⁷/₈". Cut each square once diagonally to make 108 **triangles** (**B**).
- Cut 30 strips 2¹/₈"w. From these strips, cut 540 **squares** (**C**) 2¹/₈" x 2¹/₈".
- Cut 5 strips 1³/₄"w. From these strips, cut 108 **squares** (**D**) 1³/₄" x 1³/₄".

From red solid:
- Cut 4 strips 1³/₄"w. From these strips, cut 72 **squares** (**E**) 1³/₄" x 1³/₄".
- Cut 3 strips 5⁷/₈"w. From these strips, cut 36 **rectangles** (**F**) 2¹/₄" x 5⁷/₈".
- Cut 3 strips 5⁷/₈"w. From these strips, cut 18 squares 5⁷/₈" x 5⁷/₈". Cut each square once diagonally to make 36 **triangles** (**G**).
- Cut 30 strips 2¹/₈"w. From these strips, cut 540 **squares** (**H**) 2¹/₈" x 2¹/₈".
- Cut 6 strips 2¹/₈"w. From these strips, cut 108 squares 2¹/₈" x 2¹/₈". Cut each square once diagonally to make 216 **triangles** (**I**).
- Cut 8 **binding strips** 2¹/₂"w.

YARDAGE REQUIREMENTS
Yardage is based on 43"/44" (109 cm/112 cm) wide fabric.

5¹/₂ yds (5 m) of white solid fabric

3⁵/₈ yds (3.3 m) of red solid fabric

7 yds (6.4 m) of backing fabric

⁷/₈ yd (80 cm) of binding fabric

You will also need: 84" x 84" (213 cm x 213 cm) square of batting

23

Fig. 1

Triangle-Squares
(make 1080)

Fig. 2

Unit 1 (make 36)

Unit 1 reversed
(make 36)

Unit 2 (make 36)

Unit 3 (make 36)

Unit 4 (make 36)

Unit 5 (make 36)

Unit 6 (make 36)

Unit 7 (make 36)

Unit 8 (make 36)

MAKING THE TRIANGLE-SQUARES

*Follow **Piecing and Pressing**, page 51, to assemble the quilt top.*

1. Draw diagonal line (corner to corner) on wrong side of each **square** (C). With right sides together, place 1 **square** (C) on top of 1 **square** (H). Stitch ¹/₄" on each side of drawn line (**Fig. 1**).

2. Cut along drawn line and press open to make 2 **Triangle-Squares**. Make 1080 **Triangle-Squares**.

MAKING THE BLOCKS

1. Draw a diagonal line (corner to corner) on wrong side of **squares** (E). With right sides together, place 1 **square** (E) on corner of 1 (A) as shown. Stitch on drawn line (**Fig. 2**) Trim ¹/₄" from stitching line. Open up and press seam allowances to darker fabric to make **Unit 1**. Make 36 **Unit 1's**. Sew 1 **square** (E) to 1 (A reversed) to make **Unit 1 reversed**. Make 36 **Unit 1's reversed**.

2. Sew 1 **Unit 1** and 1 **Unit 1 reversed** to 1 **rectangle** (F) to make **Unit 2**. Make 36 **Unit 2's**.

3. Sew 1 **triangle** (G) to 1 **Unit 2** to make **Unit 3**. Make 36 **Unit 3's**.

4. Sew 1 **triangle** (B) to **Unit 3** to make **Unit 4**. Make 36 **Unit 4's**.

5. Sew 3 **Triangle-Squares** and 1 **triangle** (I) together to make **Unit 5**. Make 36 **Unit 5's**.

6. Sew 4 **Triangle-Squares** and 1 **triangle** (I) together to make **Unit 6**. Make 36 **Unit 6's**.

7. Sew 5 **Triangle-Squares** and 1 **triangle** (I) together to make **Unit 7**. Make 36 **Unit 7's**.

8. Sew 1 **Unit 5**, 1 **Unit 6**, and 1 **Unit 7** together to make **Unit 8**. Make 36 **Unit 8's**.

9. Sew 1 **square (D)**, 5 **Triangle-Squares** and 1 **triangle (I)** together to make **Unit 9**. Make 36 **Unit 9's**.

10. Sew 1 **square (D)**, 6 **Triangle-Squares** and 1 **triangle (I)** together to make **Unit 10**. Make 36 **Unit 10's**.

11. Sew 1 **square (D)**, 7 **Triangle-Squares** and 1 **triangle (I)** together to make **Unit 11**. Make 36 **Unit 11's**.

12. Sew 1 **Unit 9**, 1 **Unit 10**, and 1 **Unit 11** together to make **Unit 12**. Make 36 **Unit 12's**.

Unit 9 (make 36)

Unit 10 (make 36)

Unit 11 (make 36)

Unit 12 (make 36)

"Helen couldn't believe her own eyes. For a moment she stared at the insert in the church newsletter, hoping that she just needed new glasses worse than she'd feared. But even when she squinted, the words still read the same. Quilt exhibit? They were doing an exhibit of her quilts and nobody had bothered to tell her?"
— from Wedding Ring

Unit 13 (make 36)

Block

Row

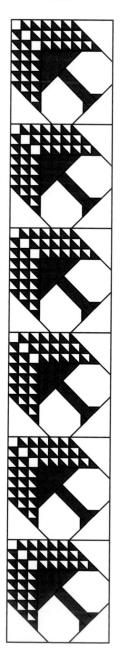

13. Sew 1 **Unit 8** and 1 **Unit 12** to **Unit 4** to make **Unit 13**. Make 36 **Unit 13's**.

14. Sew 1 **triangle (B)** to each side of **Unit 13** to complete **Block**. Make 36 **Blocks**.

ASSEMBLING THE QUILT TOP

1. Sew 6 **Blocks** together to make a vertical **Row**. Make 6 **Rows**.

2. Sew 6 **Rows** together to complete **Quilt Top**.

COMPLETING THE QUILT

1. Follow **Quilting**, page 54, to mark, layer and quilt as desired. Our quilt is hand quilted in diagonal lines approximately 1" apart across the quilt top.

2. Follow **Making Straight-Grain Binding**, page 60, to bind quilt using 2$^1/_2$"w binding.

"I don't go to quilt shows, don't go to quilt meetings. I just quilt. Don't matter to me one bit if any of my quilts see the light of day." Nancy heard the words but knew the truth beneath them. Helen was unsure of her own work, and she would never try on her own to have any of it displayed publicly. But that was what daughters were for.

— from Wedding Ring

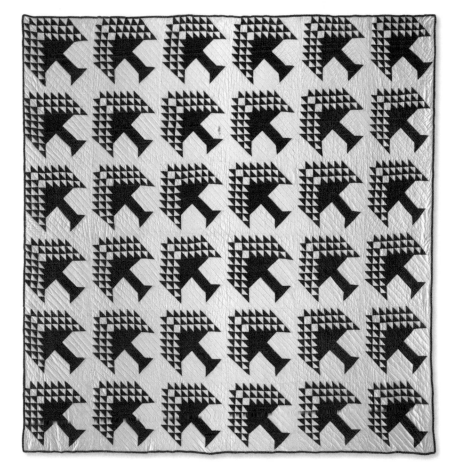

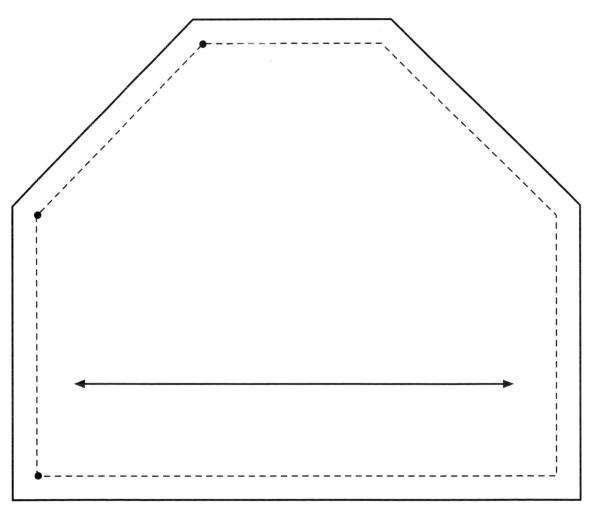

Cissy's Pinwheels

Created in sweet pastels and finished with a scalloped border, this baby quilt is pretty enough to display on a wall when it isn't wrapping a precious little one. Helen surprised her family when she volunteered to teach a neighbor, Cissy Mowrey, to quilt. The pinwheel pattern was Cissy's first choice.

Design by Bonnie Olaveson
QUILT SIZE: 45¼" x 45¼" (115 cm x 115 cm)
FINISHED BLOCK SIZE: 4¼" x 4¼" (11 cm x 11 cm)

CUTTING OUT THE PIECES

*Refer to **Rotary Cutting**, page 50, to cut strips. Cutting lengths given for borders are exact. All measurements include a $^1/_4$" seam allowance.*

From white solid:
- Cut 4 strips 3"w. From these strips, cut 50 **squares (A)** 3" x 3".
- Cut 8 **strips (B)** 1"w.
- Cut 2 **side inner narrow borders (C)** 1" x 30³/₄".
- Cut 2 **top/bottom inner narrow borders (D)** 1" x 31³/₄".
- Cut 2 **side outer narrow borders (E)** 1" x 32³/₄".
- Cut 2 **top/bottom outer narrow borders (F)** 1" x 33³/₄".

From green solid:
- Cut 16 **strips (G)** 1"w.
- Cut 2 **side middle narrow borders (H)** 1" x 31³/₄".
- Cut 2 **top/bottom middle narrow borders (I)** 1" x 32³/₄".

From green print:
- Cut 2 lengthwise **top/bottom outer wide borders (J)** 6" x 33³/₄".
- Cut 2 lengthwise **side outer wide borders (K)** 6" x 44³/₄".

From pink print:
- Cut 4 strips 3"w. From these strips, cut 50 **squares (L)** 3" x 3".

From pink plaid:
- Cut 2 strips 2"w. From these strips, cut 36 **sashing squares (M)** 2" x 2".

YARDAGE REQUIREMENTS
Yardage is based on 43"/44" (109 cm/112 cm) wide fabric.

⅞ yd (80 cm) of white solid fabric

⅝ yd (57 cm) of green solid fabric

1⅜ yds (1.3 m) of green print fabric

⅜ yd (34 cm) of pink print fabric

⅛ yd (11 cm) of pink plaid fabric

3 yds (2.7 m) of backing fabric

¾ yd (69 cm) of binding fabric

You will also need: 53" x 53" (135 cm x 135 cm) square of batting

Freezer paper

"Cissy arrived for a quilting lesson Thursday morning, and before she left, she went to show Tessa the progress she'd made on piecing her top. Clearly Cissy was taking a great deal of pride in the baby quilt, and the six pinwheel blocks she'd made so far had been sewn into a perfect rectangle."

— from Wedding Ring

Fig. 1

Triangle-Squares
(make 100)

Pinwheel Block
(make 25)

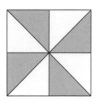

Strip Set (make 8)   **Sashing** (make 60)

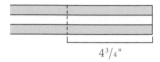 

$4^3/4$"

Row 1 (make 6)

Row 2 (make 5)

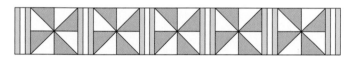

Quilt Top Center

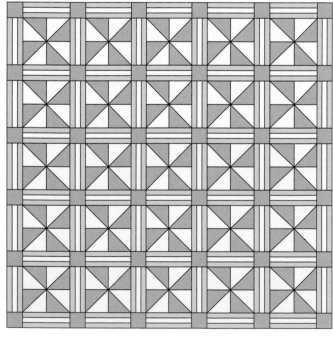

MAKING THE PINWHEEL BLOCKS

*Follow **Piecing and Pressing**, page 51, to assemble the quilt top.*

1. Draw a diagonal line (corner to corner) on wrong side of each **square** (A). With right sides together, place 1 **square** (A) on top of 1 **square** (L). Stitch $^1/_4$" on each side of drawn line (**Fig. 1**).

2. Cut along drawn line and press open to make 2 **Triangle-Squares**. Make 100 **Triangle-Squares**.

3. Sew 4 **Triangle-Squares** together to make **Pinwheel Block**. Make 25 **Pinwheel Blocks**.

MAKING THE SASHINGS

1. Sew 2 **strips** (G) and 1 **strip** (B) together into a **Strip Set**. Make 8 **Strip Sets**. Cut across Strip Sets at $4^3/4$" intervals to make a total of 60 **Sashings**.

ASSEMBLING THE QUILT TOP CENTER

1. Sew 6 **sashing squares** (M) and 5 **Sashings** together to make **Row 1**. Make 6 **Row 1's**.

2. Sew 6 **Sashings** and 5 **Pinwheel Blocks** together to make **Row 2**. Make 5 **Row 2's**.

3. Sew **Row 1's** and **Row 2's** together to make **Quilt Top Center**.

ADDING THE BORDERS

1. Sew 1 **side inner narrow border** (C) to each side of Quilt Top Center.

2. Sew 1 **top/bottom inner narrow border** (D) to top and bottom of Quilt Top Center.

3. Sew 1 **side middle narrow border** (H) to each side of Quilt Top Center.

4. Sew 1 **top/bottom middle narrow border** (I) to top and bottom of Quilt Top Center.

5. Sew 1 **side outer narrow border** (E) to each side of Quilt Top Center.

6. Sew 1 **top/bottom outer narrow border** (F) to top and bottom of Quilt Top Center.

7. Sew 1 **top/bottom outer wide border (J)** to top and bottom of Quilt Top Center.

8. Sew 1 **side outer wide border (K)** to each side of Quilt Top Center.

9. Trace Corner Scallop pattern onto dull side of freezer paper; cut out along traced line. Placing straight edge of pattern on border seam, iron the corner scallop pattern to one corner of the Quilt Top. Trace around the scallop with a fabric-marking pen. Repeat for remaining corners of Quilt Top.

10. Trace Scallop pattern onto dull side of freezer paper; cut out along traced line. Placing long, straight edge of pattern on border seam and matching repeat lines, iron the pattern to the Quilt Top. Trace around the scallop with a fabric-marking pen. Repeat along 1 side of Quilt Top. Repeat for remaining sides of Quilt Top.

COMPLETING THE QUILT

1. Follow **Quilting**, page 54, to mark, layer and quilt as desired. Our quilt is outline quilted around each pinwheel and sashing square and meander quilted in all other areas.

2. To prepare quilt for binding, Straight Stitch around quilt on drawn line. Trim borders $1/8$" outside stitching line.

3. Cut a 24" square of binding fabric. Follow **Making Continuous Bias Binding**, page 59, to make $2^1/2$"w bias binding. Press one end of binding diagonally.

4. Follow **Attaching Binding with Mitered Corners**, page 60, Step 1 to pin binding to front of quilt, easing binding around curved edges. Sew binding to quilt until binding overlaps beginning end by approximately 1". Trim excess binding. Fold binding over to quilt backing and pin in place, covering stitching line. Blindstitch binding to backing.

Scallop

fold

Corner Scallop
To make whole pattern, fold freezer paper in half with dull side out. Place fold of freezer paper on fold of pattern. Trace pattern along solid line. Turn freezer paper over and trace previously drawn line. Unfold freezer paper.

Helen's Star

Helen alternated Spinning Star blocks with Nine-Patch blocks to bring this pastel creation to life. The gentle hues may remind viewers of Easter or springtime, as well as the sweetness of a new baby.

Design by Bonnie Olaveson
QUILT SIZE: 45" x 45" (114 cm x 114 cm)
FINISHED BLOCK SIZE: 4⅞" x 4⅞" (12 cm x 12 cm)

CUTTING OUT THE PIECES

*Refer to **Rotary Cutting**, page 50, to cut strips. Cutting lengths given for borders are exact. All measurements include a ¹/₄" seam allowance.*

From white solid:
- Cut 4 strips 2¹/₂"w. From these strips, cut 58 **squares (A)** 2¹/₂" x 2¹/₂".
- Cut 12 strips 2¹/₈"w. From these strips, cut 212 **squares (B)** 2¹/₈" x 2¹/₈".

From yellow print:
- Cut 4 strips 2¹/₂"w. From these strips, cut 58 **squares (C)** 2¹/₂" x 2¹/₂".
- Cut 2 strips 2¹/₈"w. From these strips, cut 29 **squares (D)** 2¹/₈" x 2¹/₈".

From assorted prints and solids:
- Cut 120 **squares (E)** 2¹/₈" x 2¹/₈".

From blue print, peach plaid, and green solid:
- Cut 4 **Border Strips (F)** 2¹/₈" x 34⁵/₈" from **each** fabric.

From binding fabric:
- Cut 5 strips 2¹/₂"w.

YARDAGE REQUIREMENTS
Yardage is based on 43"/44" (109 cm/112 cm) wide fabric.

1¹/₈ yd (1 m) of white solid fabric

¹/₂ yd (46 cm) of yellow print fabric

¹/₂ yd (46 cm) **total** of assorted print and solid fabrics for 9-Patch blocks

¹/₄ yd (23 cm) **each** of blue print, peach plaid, and green solid fabrics for borders

3 yds (2.7 m) of backing fabric

¹/₂ yd (46 cm) of binding fabric

You will also need: 53" x 53" (135 cm x 135 cm) rectangle of batting

Fig. 1

Triangle-Square (make 116)

Unit 1 (make 58)   Unit 2 (make 29)

Star Block (make 29)

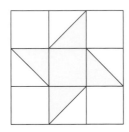

Unit 3 (make 48)   Unit 4 (make 24)

9-Patch Block (make 24)

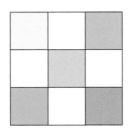

Row A (make 4)

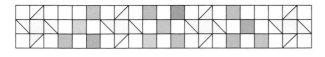

Row B (make 3)

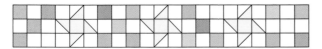

MAKING THE TRIANGLE-SQUARES

*Follow **Piecing and Pressing**, page 51, to assemble the quilt top.*

1. Draw a diagonal line (corner to corner) on wrong side of each **square (A)**. With right sides together, place 1 **square (A)** on top of 1 **square (C)**. Stitch $1/4$" on each side of drawn line (**Fig. 1**).

2. Cut along drawn line and press open to make 2 **Triangle-Squares**. Make 116 **Triangle-Squares**.

MAKING THE STAR BLOCKS

1. Sew 2 **squares (B)** and 1 **Triangle-Square** together to make **Unit 1**. Make 58 **Unit 1's**.

2. Sew 1 **square (D)** and 2 **Triangle-Squares** together to make **Unit 2**. Make 29 **Unit 2's**.

3. Sew 2 **Unit 1's** and 1 **Unit 2** together to make **Star Block**. Make 29 **Star Blocks**.

MAKING THE 9-PATCH BLOCKS

1. Sew 2 **squares (E)** and 1 **Square (B)** together to make **Unit 3**. Make 48 **Unit 3's**.

2. Sew 2 **squares (B)** and 1 **Square (E)** together to make **Unit 4**. Make 24 **Unit 4's**.

3. Sew 2 **Unit 3's** and 1 **Unit 4** together to make **9-Patch Block**. Make 24 **9-Patch Blocks**.

ASSEMBLING THE QUILT TOP CENTER

1. Sew 4 **Star Blocks** and 3 **9-Patch Blocks** together to make **Row A**. Make 4 **Row A's**.

2. Sew 4 **9-Patch Blocks** and 3 **Star Blocks** together to make **Row B**. Make 3 **Row B's**.

3. Sew **Row A's** and **Row B's** together to make **Quilt Top Center**.

ADDING THE BORDERS

1. Sew 1 **blue print border strip** (**F**), 1 **peach plaid border strip** (**F**), and 1 **green solid border strip** (**F**) together to make **Border**. Make 4 **Borders**.

2. Sew 1 **Border** to each side of Quilt Top Center.

3. Sew 1 **Star Block** to each end of remaining **Borders**.

4. Sew remaining **Borders** to top and bottom of Quilt Top Center.

COMPLETING THE QUILT

1. Follow **Quilting**, page 54, to mark, layer and quilt as desired. Our quilt is machine meander quilted.

2. Follow **Making Straight-Grain Binding**, page 60, to make binding.

3. Follow **Attaching Binding with Mitered Corners**, page 60, to attach binding.

"Your grandmother used to make quilts for every baby at church, even if the family was brand new in town. And if somebody got burned out or their house got flooded, Mama was right there with quilts."
— *Nancy Whitlock*,
Wedding Ring

Simple Pleasures

If this fun creation reminds you of fingerpaints and coloring crayons, you're not alone. The playful whirl of bright Bowtie or Hourglass Blocks invites the viewer to find enjoyment in simple things … like creating a Simple Pleasures Quilt. Helen certainly enjoys creating baby quilts of all kinds, even though she claims to dislike children.

Design by Bonnie Olaveson
QUILT SIZE: 64$\frac{1}{4}$" x 64$\frac{1}{4}$" (163 cm x 163 cm)
FINISHED BLOCK SIZE: Hourglass Block — 4$\frac{1}{4}$" x 4$\frac{1}{4}$" (11 cm x 11 cm),
Star Block — 4$\frac{7}{8}$" x 4$\frac{7}{8}$" (12 cm x 12 cm)

CUTTING OUT THE PIECES

*Refer to **Rotary Cutting**, page 50, to cut strips. Cutting lengths given for borders are exact. All measurements include a $^1/_4$" seam allowance.*

From assorted white prints:
- Cut 50 **squares** (A) $5^1/_2$" x $5^1/_2$".

From assorted colored prints:
- Cut 50 **squares** (B) $5^1/_2$" x $5^1/_2$".

From yellow print:
- Cut 4 **inner border strips** (C) $2^1/_8$" x 43", pieced as needed.
- Cut 1 strip $2^1/_2$"w. From this strip, cut 8 **squares** (D) $2^1/_2$" x $2^1/_2$".
- Cut 1 strip $2^1/_8$"w. From this strip, cut 4 **squares** (E) $2^1/_8$" x $2^1/_8$".

From blue print:
- Cut 4 **inner border strips** (F) $2^1/_8$" x 43", pieced as needed.
- Cut 1 strip $2^1/_2$"w. From this strip, cut 8 **squares** (G) $2^1/_2$" x $2^1/_2$".
- Cut 1 strip $2^1/_8$"w. From this strip, cut 16 **squares** (H) $2^1/_8$" x $2^1/_8$".

From green print:
- Cut 4 **inner border strips** (I) $2^1/_8$" x 43", pieced as needed.

From red print:
- Cut 2 lengthwise **side outer borders** (J) 6" x $52^3/_4$".
- Cut 2 lengthwise **top/bottom outer borders** (K) 6" x $63^3/_4$".

From binding fabric:
- Cut 7 **strips** $2^1/_2$"w.

YARDAGE REQUIREMENTS
Yardage is based on 43"/44" (109 cm/112 cm) wide fabric.

$1^3/_8$ yds (1.3 m) **total** of assorted white print fabrics for Hourglass Blocks

$1^3/_8$ yds (1.3 m) **total** of assorted colored print fabrics for Hourglass Blocks

$^1/_2$ yd (46 cm) **each** of yellow print, blue print, and green print fabric for inner border

2 yds (1.8 m) of red print fabric for outer border

4 yds (3.7 m) of backing fabric

$^5/_8$ yd (57 cm) of binding fabric

You will also need: 72" x 72" (183 cm x 183 cm) rectangle of batting

Fig. 1

Triangle-Square A
(make 100)

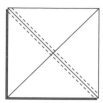 

Fig. 2

Hourglass Blocks
(make 100)

Fig. 3

Triangle-Square B's
(make 16)

Unit 1 (make 8)   **Unit 2** (make 4)

Star Block (make 4)

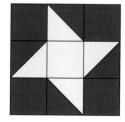

MAKING THE HOURGLASS BLOCKS

*Follow **Piecing and Pressing**, page 51, to assemble the quilt top.*

1. Draw a diagonal line (corner to corner) in both directions on wrong side of each **square (A)**. With right sides together, place 1 **square (A)** on top of 1 **square (B)**. Stitch 1/4" from each side of 1 drawn line (**Fig. 1**).

2. Cut along drawn line and press open to make 2 **Triangle-Square A's**. Make 100 **Triangle-Square A's**.

3. On wrong side of 50 **Triangle-Square A's**, extend drawn line from corner of white print triangle to corner of colored print triangle.

4. Match 1 *marked* **Triangle-Square A** and 1 *unmarked* **Triangle-Square A** with white triangles opposite each other and marked unit on top. Stitch 1/4" from each side of drawn line (**Fig. 2**). Cut apart along drawn line to make 2 **Hourglass Blocks**; press Units open. Make 100 **Hourglass Blocks**.

MAKING THE STAR BLOCKS

1. Draw a diagonal line (corner to corner) on wrong side of each **square (D)**. With right sides together, place 1 **square (D)** on top of 1 **square (G)**. Stitch 1/4" on each side of drawn line (**Fig. 3**).

2. Cut along drawn line and press open to make 2 **Triangle-Square B's**. Make 16 **Triangle-Square B's**.

3. Sew 2 **squares (H)** and 1 **Triangle-Square B** together to make **Unit 1**. Make 8 **Unit 1's**.

4. Sew 1 **square (E)** and 2 **Triangle-Squares** together to make **Unit 2**. Make 4 **Unit 2's**.

5. Sew 2 **Unit 1's** and 1 **Unit 2** together to make **Star Block**. Make 4 **Star Blocks**.

ASSEMBLING THE QUILT TOP CENTER

1. Rotating every other block, sew 10 **Hourglass Blocks** together to make **Row**. Make 10 **Rows**.

2. Rotating every other Row, sew **Rows** together to make **Quilt Top Center**.

Row (make 10)

Quilt Top Center

ADDING THE BORDERS

1. Sew 1 **inner border strip (F)**, 1 **inner border strip (C)**, and 1 **inner border strip (I)** together to make **Inner Border**. Make 4 **Inner Borders**.

2. Sew 1 **Inner Border** to each side of Quilt Top Center.

3. Sew 1 **Star Block** to each end of remaining **Inner Border**.

4. Sew remaining **Inner Borders** to top and bottom of Quilt Top Center.

5. Sew 1 **Side Outer Border (J)** to each side of Quilt Top Center.

6. Sew **Top/Bottom Outer Borders (K)** to top and bottom of Quilt Top Center.

COMPLETING THE QUILT

1. Follow **Quilting**, page 54, to mark, layer and quilt as desired. Our quilt is machine quilted with swirls in the Hourglass Blocks, pointed petals in the Star Blocks, loops in the Inner Border, and loops and stars in the Outer Border.

2. Follow **Making Straight-Grain Binding**, page 60, to make binding.

3. Follow **Attaching Binding with Mitered Corners**, page 60, to attach binding.

"'Feed sacks.' Tessa smiled, delighted she'd been able to make the identification. Someone, perhaps her grandmother, had taken out the stitching that made this rectangle a bag. Then the fabric had been washed and ironed and folded for future use. Tessa imagined the woman who had folded it going to the store and choosing this particular flour or chicken feed sack because of color or pattern, knowing that she would use it someday to clothe her family or keep them warm. Women with very little not only making do, but making art as they did."

— Tessa MacCrae, Wedding Ring

Rayley's Sunbonnet Sue

Little girls in big bonnets have been a popular appliqué theme for almost a century. These six Sunbonnet Sue Blocks show Sue in some of her classic activities, such as petting a cat, building a sandcastle, and jumping rope. Helen modified her blocks to feature the activities that her great-grandchild enjoyed most.

FINISHED BLOCK SIZE: 9" x 9" (23 cm x 23 cm)

Make as many of these sweet Sunbonnet Sue blocks as you desire. Use your blocks to make a beautiful wall hanging, baby quilt, or bed quilt. Choose fabrics in colors to appeal to your favorite little girl. Embellish the blocks with embroidery, buttons, and trims. Simply set them together with sashings and sashing squares (if desired) and add borders.

MAKING THE BLOCKS

*Refer to **Preparing Fusible Appliqués**, page 52, and use patterns, pages 44-49, to cut and place appliqués.*

1. Refer to **Almost Invisible Appliqué**, page 53, to fuse and appliqué blocks. Trim blocks to 9¹/₂" x 9¹/₂".

2. Follow table, below, and **Hand Stitches**, page 62, to add embellishments and embroidery details using 2 strands of floss. The embroidery details are shown on the patterns for guidance.

	Embroidery Detail	Embellishments
Picking Flowers	Stem Stitch flower stems green Satin Stitch leaves green	Buttons for flowers
Rainy Day	Satin Stitch umbrella handle black Backstitch umbrella details black Satin Stitch raindrops blue Running Stitch puddle blue	Buttons on coat Frog button in puddle
Cat	Backstitch eyes, mouth, whiskers black Satin Stitch nose black Running Stitch detail on apron black	Ribbon sewn to hat for hatband Ribbon bow sewn to hat Floss bow sewn to cat
Birds	Satin Stitch birds blue Straight Stitch beaks and legs black French Knot bird eyes black French Knot detail on apron blue	Button in center of bow Button for birdhouse door
Jump Rope	Backstitch rope black	Red heart buttons on dress Lace sewn at dress hem
Sandcastle	Satin Stitch flag yellow Running Stitch door black Backstitch sand and feet detail black	Yellow star buttons Button in center of bow Ribbon sewn to hat for hatband

YARDAGE REQUIREMENTS

10¹/₂" x 10¹/₂" (27 cm x 27 cm) square of background fabric for each block

Scraps of fabric for appliqués

You will also need:
Paper-backed fusible web

Stabilizer

Clear nylon thread

Embroidery floss

Desired embellishments

Key:
Thick black lines indicate cutting lines.
Thin black lines or dots indicate embroidery detail.
Grey lines indicate appliqué placement or overlap.

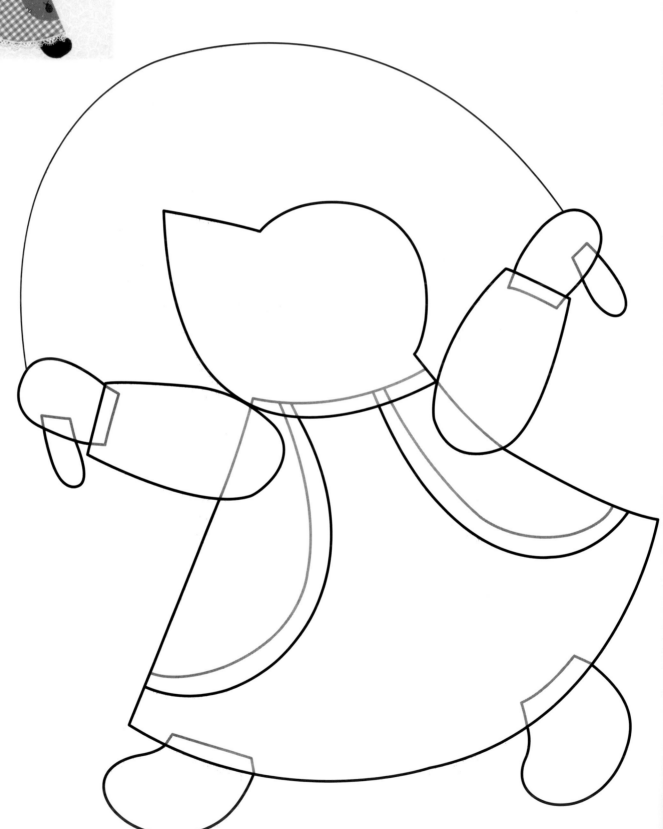

46

General Instructions

Complete instructions are given for making each of the projects shown in this book. To make your project easier and more enjoyable, we encourage you to carefully read all the general instructions, study the color photographs, and familiarize yourself with the individual project instructions before beginning a project.

ROTARY CUTTING

Rotary cutting has brought speed and accuracy to quiltmaking by allowing quilters to easily cut strips of fabric and then cut those strips into smaller pieces.

Fig. 1

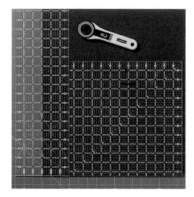

- Place fabric on work surface with fold closest to you.

- Cut all strips from the selvage-to-selvage width of the fabric unless otherwise indicated in project instructions.

- Square left edge of fabric using rotary cutter and rulers (**Figs. 1 - 2**).

- To cut each strip required for a project, place the ruler over the cut edge of the fabric, aligning desired marking on the ruler with the cut edge (**Fig. 3**); make the cut.

- When cutting several strips from a single piece of fabric, it is important to make sure that cuts remain at a perfect right angle to the fold; square fabric as needed.

Fig. 2

TEMPLATE CUTTING

Our piecing template patterns include a ¹/₄" seam allowance. Patterns for appliqué templates do not include seam allowances. When cutting instructions say to cut in reverse, place the template upside down on the fabric to cut piece in reverse.

1. To make a template from a pattern, use a permanent fine-point pen to carefully trace the pattern onto template plastic, making sure to transfer all markings. Cut out template along outer drawn line. Check template against original pattern for accuracy.

Fig. 3

2. To use a piecing template, place template on wrong side of fabric (unless otherwise indicated), aligning grain line on template with straight grain of fabric. Use a sharp fabric marking pencil to draw around template. Cut out fabric piece using scissors or rotary cutting equipment.

3. To use appliqué templates, place template on right side of fabric. Use a mechanical pencil with a very fine lead to draw around template on fabric. Use scissors to cut out appliqué a scant ¹/₄" outside drawn line.

PIECING AND PRESSING

Precise cutting, followed by accurate piecing and careful pressing, will ensure that all the pieces of your quilt top fit together well.

PIECING

- Set sewing machine stitch length for approximately 11 stitches per inch.

- Use a neutral-colored general-purpose sewing thread (not quilting thread) in the needle and in the bobbin.

- An accurate $^1/_4$" seam allowance is *essential*. Presser feet that are $^1/_4$" wide are available for most sewing machines.

- When piecing, always place pieces **right sides** together and match raw edges; pin if necessary.

- Chain piecing saves time and will usually result in more accurate piecing.

- Trim away points of seam allowances that extend beyond edges of sewn seams.

Sewing Across Seam Intersections

When sewing across the intersection of two seams, place pieces right sides together and match seams exactly, making sure seam allowances are pressed in opposite directions (**Fig. 4**).

Sewing Strip Sets

When there are several strips to assemble into a strip set, first sew the strips together into pairs, then sew the pairs together to form the strip set. To help avoid distortion, sew 1 seam in 1 direction and then sew the next seam in the opposite direction (**Fig. 5**).

Fig. 4

Fig. 5

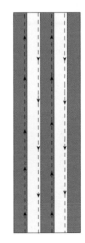

PRESSING

- Use a steam iron set on "Cotton" for all pressing.

- Press after sewing each seam.

- Seam allowances are almost always pressed to one side, usually toward the darker fabric. However, to reduce bulk it may occasionally be necessary to press seam allowances toward the lighter fabric or even to press them open.

- To prevent a dark fabric seam allowance from showing through a light fabric, trim the darker seam allowance slightly narrower than the lighter seam allowance.

- To press long seams, such as those in long strip sets, without curving or other distortion, lay strips across the width of the ironing board.

APPLIQUÉ
Needle-Turn Appliqué

In this traditional hand appliqué method, the needle is used to turn the seam allowance under as you sew the appliqué to the background fabric using a Blind Stitch, page 62 (Fig. 39). When stitching, match the color of thread to the color of appliqué to disguise your stitches. Appliqué each piece starting with the ones directly on the background fabric. It is not necessary to appliqué areas that will be covered by another appliqué. Stitches on the right side of fabric should not show. Clipped areas should be secured with a few extra stitches to prevent fraying.

1. Place template on right side of appliqué fabric. Use a mechanical pencil with a very fine lead to lightly draw around template, leaving at least $1/2$" between shapes; repeat for number of appliqués specified in project instructions.

2. Cut out shapes a scant $1/4$" outside drawn line. Arrange shapes on background fabric and pin or baste in place.

3. Thread a sharps needle with a single strand of general-purpose sewing thread the color of the appliqué; knot one end.

4. Pin center of appliqué to right side of background fabric. Begin on as straight an edge as possible and use point of needle to turn under a small amount of seam allowance, concealing drawn line on appliqué. Blindstitch appliqué to the background, turning under the seam allowance. Clip inside curves and points up to, but not through, drawn line as you stitch.

Preparing Fusible Appliqués

Patterns for fused appliqués are printed in reverse to enable you to use our speedy method of preparing appliqués by following Steps 1 – 3 (below). White or light-colored fabrics may need to be lined with fusible interfacing before applying fusible web to prevent darker fabrics from showing through.

1. Place paper-backed fusible web, web side down, over appliqué pattern. Use a pencil to trace pattern onto paper side of web as many times as indicated in project instructions for a single fabric.

2. Follow manufacturer's instructions to fuse traced patterns to wrong side of fabrics. Do not remove paper backing.

3. Use scissors to cut out appliqué pieces along traced lines. Remove paper backing from all pieces.

Almost Invisible Appliqué

In this variation of Satin Stitch appliqué, transparent nylon thread is used to secure the appliqué pieces. Transparent nylon thread is available in two colors: clear and smoke. Clear is used on white or very light fabrics and smoke on darker colors.

Fig. 6

1. Pin stabilizer, such as paper or any of the commercially available products, on wrong side of background fabric before stitching appliqués in place.

Fig. 7

2. Thread sewing machine with transparent nylon thread; use general-purpose thread that matches background fabric in bobbin.

3. Set sewing machine for a narrow zigzag stitch and a short to medium stitch length, depending on desired look. Slightly loosening the top tension may yield a smoother stitch.

Fig. 8

4. Begin by stitching two or three stitches in place (drop feed dogs or set stitch length at 0) to anchor thread. Most of the Satin Stitch should be on the appliqué with the right edge of the stitch falling at the outside edge of the appliqué. Stitch over all exposed raw edges of appliqué pieces.

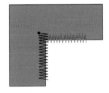
Fig. 9

5. *(Note: Dots on Figs. 6 – 11 indicate where to leave needle in fabric when pivoting.)* For outside corners, stitch just past corner, stopping with needle in background fabric (**Fig. 6**). Raise presser foot. Pivot project, lower presser foot, and stitch adjacent side (**Fig. 7**).

6. For inside corners, stitch just past corner, stopping with needle in appliqué fabric (**Fig. 8**). Raise presser foot. Pivot project, lower presser foot, and stitch adjacent side (**Fig. 9**).

Fig. 10

7. When stitching outside curves, stop with needle in background fabric. Raise presser foot and pivot project as needed. Lower presser foot and continue stitching, pivoting as often as necessary to follow curve (**Fig. 10**).

8. When stitching inside curves, stop with needle in appliqué fabric. Raise presser foot and pivot project as needed. Lower presser foot and continue stitching, pivoting as often as necessary to follow curve (**Fig. 11**).

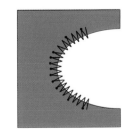
Fig. 11

9. Do not backstitch at end of stitching. Pull threads to wrong side of background fabric; know thread and trim ends.

10. Carefully tear away stabilizer.

QUILTING

Quilting holds the 3 layers (top, batting, and backing) of the quilt together and can be done by hand or machine. Because marking, layering, and quilting are interrelated and may be done in different orders depending on circumstances, please read the entire **Quilting** *section, pages 54 - 58, before beginning project.*

TYPES OF QUILTING

In the Ditch Quilting
Quilting along seamlines or along edges of appliquéd pieces is called "in the ditch" quilting. This type of quilting should be done on the side **opposite** the seam allowance and does not need to be marked.

Outline Quilting
Quilting a consistent distance, usually $1/4$", from a seam or appliqué is called "outline" quilting. Outline quilting may be marked, or $1/4$"w masking tape may be placed along seamlines for a quilting guide. (Do not leave tape on quilt longer than necessary, since it may leave an adhesive residue.)

Motif Quilting
Quilting a design, such as a feathered wreath is called "motif" quilting. This type of quilting should be marked before basting quilt layers together.

Echo Quilting
Quilting that follows the outline of an appliquéd or pieced design with 2 or more parallel lines is called "echo" quilting. This type of quilting does not need to be marked.

Channel Quilting
Quilting with straight, parallel lines is called "channel" quilting. This type of quilting may be marked or stitched using a guide.

Crosshatch Quilting
Quilting straight lines in a grid pattern is called "crosshatch" quilting. Lines may be stitched parallel to edges of quilt or stitched diagonally. This type of quilting may be marked or stitched using a guide.

Meandering Quilting
Quilting in random curved lines and swirls is called "meandering" quilting. Quilting lines should not cross or touch each other. This type of quilting does not need to be marked.

Stipple Quilting
Meandering quilting that is very closely spaced is called "stipple" quilting. Stippling will flatten the area quilted and is often stitched in background areas to raise appliquéd or pieced designs. This type of quilting does not need to be marked.

"Tessa wished Kayley were there in the attic with her, to see the quilt that Tessa had never thought to mention to her daughter, to hear the stories of Tessa's own childhood. She laid her cheek against the disintegrating cotton."
— from Wedding Ring

MARKING QUILTING LINES

Quilting lines may be marked using fabric marking pencils, chalk markers, water- or air-soluble pens, or lead pencils.

Simple quilting designs may be marked with chalk or chalk pencil after basting. A small area may be marked, then quilted, before moving to next area to be marked. Intricate designs should be marked before basting using a more durable marker.

Caution: Pressing may permanently set some marks. Test different markers **on scrap fabric** to find one that marks clearly and can be thoroughly removed.

A wide variety of precut quilting stencils, as well as entire books of quilting patterns, are available. Using a stencil makes it easier to mark intricate or repetitive designs on your quilt top.

To make a stencil from a pattern, center template plastic over pattern and use a permanent marker to trace pattern onto plastic. Use a craft knife with a single or double blade to cut narrow slits along traced lines (**Fig. 12**). Use desired marking tool and stencil to mark quilting lines.

CHOOSING AND PREPARING THE BACKING

To allow for slight shifting of the quilt top during quilting, the backing should be approximately 4" larger on all sides than the quilt top for bed-sized quilts and large wall hangings and 2" larger on all sides for small wall hangings. Yardage requirements listed for quilt backings are calculated for 43"/44"w fabric. If you are making a bed-size quilt, using 90"w or 108"w fabric for the backing may eliminate piecing. To piece a backing using 45"w fabric, use the following instructions.

1. Measure length and width of quilt top; add 8" (4") to each measurement.

2. Cut the backing fabric into 2 lengths slightly longer than the determined length measurement. Trim selvages. Place lengths with right sides facing and sew long edges together, forming a tube (**Fig. 13**). Match seams and press along 1 fold (**Fig. 14**). Cut along pressed fold to form a single piece (**Fig. 15**).

3. Trim backing to correct size, if necessary, and press seam allowances open.

Fig. 12

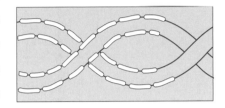

Fig. 13

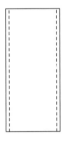

Fig. 14

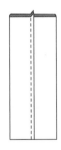

Fig. 15

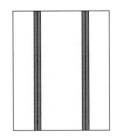

"Helen planned to quilt the wedding ring quilt herself, just as soon as it was finished. She had pieced more than two thirds of the oval sections since she first learned to quilt, but she had been choosy about fabrics, only using those she really liked or those with sentimental meaning. She was in no hurry though, because the man she wanted to marry hadn't yet asked her."
— from Wedding Ring

CHOOSING AND PREPARING THE BATTING

Choosing the right batting will make your quilting job easier. If machine quilting, choose a low-loft all cotton or a cotton/polyester blend batting because the cotton helps "grip" the layers of the quilt. For hand quilting, choose a low-loft batting in any of the fiber types described here.

Batting options include cotton/polyester batting, which combines the best of both polyester and cotton battings; fusible battings which do not need to be basted before quilting; bonded polyester which is treated with a protective coating to stabilize the fibers and to reduce "bearding," a process in which batting fibers work their way out through the quilt fabrics; and wool and silk battings, which are generally more expensive and usually only dry-cleanable.

Whichever batting you choose, read the manufacturer's instructions closely for any special notes on care or preparation. When you're ready to use your chosen batting in a project, cut batting the same size as the prepared backing.

ASSEMBLING THE QUILT

1. Examine wrong side of quilt top closely; trim any seam allowances and clip any threads that may show through to the front of the quilt. Press quilt top.

2. If quilt top is to be marked before layering, mark quilting lines (see **Marking Quilting Lines**, page 55).

3. Place backing wrong side up on a flat surface. Use masking tape to tape edges of backing to surface. Place batting on top of backing fabric. Smooth batting gently, being careful not to stretch or tear. Center quilt top right side up on batting.

4. If hand quilting, begin in the center and work toward the outer edges to hand baste all layers together. Use long stitches and place basting lines approximately 4" apart (**Fig. 16**). Smooth fullness or wrinkles toward outer edges.

5. If machine quilting, use 1" rustproof safety pins to "pin-baste" all layers together, spacing pins approximately 4" apart. Begin at the center and work toward the outer edges to secure all layers. If possible, place pins away from areas that will be quilted, although pins may be removed as needed when quilting.

HAND QUILTING

The quilting stitch is a basic running stitch that forms a broken line on the quilt top and backing. Stitches on the quilt top and backing should be straight and equal in length.

1. Secure center of quilt in hoop or frame. Check quilt top and backing to make sure they are smooth. To help prevent puckers, always begin quilting in the center of the quilt and work toward the outside edges.

2. Thread needle with an 18"-20" length of quilting thread; knot 1 end. Using a thimble, insert needle into quilt top and batting approximately ¹/₂" from where you wish to begin quilting. Bring needle up at the point where you wish to begin (**Fig. 17**); when knot catches on quilt top, give thread a quick, short pull to "pop" knot through fabric into batting (**Fig. 18**).

3. Holding the needle with your sewing hand and placing your other hand underneath the quilt, use thimble to push the tip of the needle down through all layers. As soon as needle touches your finger underneath, use that finger to push the tip of the needle only back up through the layers to top of quilt. (The amount of the needle showing above the fabric determines the length of the quilting stitch.) Referring to **Fig. 19**, rock the needle up and down, taking 3 - 6 stitches before bringing the needle and thread completely through the layers. Check the back of the quilt to make sure stitches are going through all layers. When quilting through a seam allowance or quilting a curve or corner, you may need to make 1 stitch at a time.

4. When you reach the end of your thread, knot thread close to the fabric and "pop" knot into batting; clip thread close to fabric.

5. Stop and move your hoop as often as necessary. You do not have to tie a knot every time you move your hoop; you may leave the thread dangling and pick it up again when you return to that part of the quilt.

Fig. 16

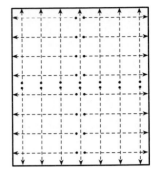

Fig. 17

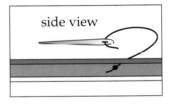
side view

Fig. 18

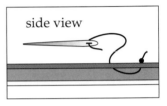
side view

Fig. 19

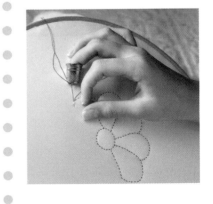

STRAIGHT-LINE MACHINE QUILTING

The following instructions are for straight-line quilting, which requires a walking foot or even-feed foot. The term "straight-line" is somewhat deceptive, since curves (especially gentle ones) as well as straight lines can be stitched with this technique.

1. Using the same color general-purpose thread in the needle and bobbin avoids "dots" of bobbin thread being pulled to the surface.

2. Using general-purpose thread, which matches the backing in the bobbin, will add pattern and dimension to the quilt back without adding contrasting color. Refer to your owner's manual for recommended tension settings.

3. Set the stitch length for 6 – 10 stitches per inch and attach the walking foot to sewing machine.

4. After pin-basting, decide which section of the quilt will have the longest continuous quilting line, oftentimes the area from center top to center bottom. Leaving the area exposed where you will place your first line of quilting, roll up each edge of the quilt to help reduce the bulk, keeping fabrics smooth. Smaller projects may not need to be rolled.

5. Start stitching at beginning of longest quilting line, using very short stitches for the first $^1/_4$" to "lock" beginning of quilting line. Stitch across project, using one hand on each side of the walking foot to slightly spread the fabric and to guide the fabric through the machine. Lock stitches at end of quilting line.

6. Continue machine quilting, stitching longer quilting lines first to stabilize the quilt before moving on to other areas.

FREE-MOTION MACHINE QUILTING

Free-motion quilting may be free-form or may follow a marked quilting pattern.

1. Using the same color general-purpose thread in the needle and bobbin avoids "dots" of bobbin thread being pulled to the surface. Use general-purpose thread in the bobbin and decorative thread for stitching, such as metallic, variegated or contrasting-colored general-purpose thread, when you desire the quilting to be more pronounced.

2. Use a darning foot and drop or cover feed dogs. Pull up bobbin thread and hold both thread ends while you stitch 2 or 3 stitches in place to lock thread. Cut threads near quilt surface.

3. Place hands lightly on quilt on either side of darning foot to slightly spread fabric and to move fabric through the machine. Even stitch length is achieved by using smooth, flowing hand motion and steady machine speed. Slow machine speed and fast hand movement will create long stitches. Fast machine speed and slow hand movement will create short stitches. Move quilt sideways, back and forth, in a circular motion, or in a random motion to create the desired designs; do not rotate quilt. Lock stitches at the end of each quilting line.

MAKING A HANGING SLEEVE

Attaching a hanging sleeve to the back of your wall hanging or quilt before the binding is added allows you to display your completed project on a wall.

1. Measure width of quilt top edge and subtract 1". Cut piece of fabric 7" wide by the determined measurement.

2. Press short edges of fabric piece $^1/_4$" to wrong side; press edges $^1/_4$" to wrong side again and machine stitch in place.

3. Matching wrong sides, fold piece in half lengthwise to form a tube.

4. Match raw edges and stitch hanging sleeve to center top edge on back of wall hanging.

5. Bind wall hanging, treating the hanging sleeve as part of the backing.

6. Blind stitch bottom of hanging sleeve to backing, taking care not to stitch through to front of quilt.

BINDING

Binding encloses the raw edges of your quilt. Because of its stretchiness, bias binding works well for binding projects with curves or rounded corners and tends to lie smooth and flat in any given circumstance. It is also more durable than other types of binding.

MAKING CONTINUOUS BIAS BINDING

Bias strips for binding can simply be cut and pieced to the desired length. However, when a long length of binding is needed, the "continuous" method is quick and accurate.

1. Cut a square from binding fabric the size indicated in the project instructions. Cut square in half diagonally to make 2 triangles.

2. With right sides together and using a $^1/_4$" seam allowance, sew triangles together (**Fig. 20**); press seam allowance open.

3. On wrong side of fabric, draw lines the width of the binding as specified in the project instructions, usually $2^1/_2$" (**Fig. 21**). Cut off any remaining fabric less than this width.

4. With right sides inside, bring short edges together to form a tube; match raw edges so that first drawn line of top section meets second drawn line of bottom section (**Fig. 22**).

5. Carefully pin edges together by inserting pins through drawn lines at the point where drawn lines intersect, making sure the pins go through intersections on both sides. Using a $^1/_4$" seam allowance, sew edges together. Press seam allowance open.

6. To cut continuous strip, begin cutting along first drawn line (**Fig. 23**). Continue cutting along drawn line around tube.

Fig. 20

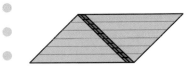

Fig. 21

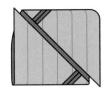

Fig. 22

Fig. 23

Fig. 24

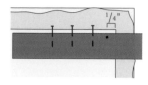

Fig. 25

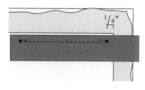

Fig. 26

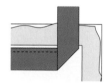

Fig. 27

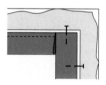

Fig. 28

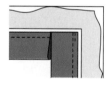

Fig. 29

Fig. 30

7.   Trim ends of bias strip square.

8.   Matching wrong sides and raw edges, press bias strip in half lengthwise to complete binding.

MAKING STRAIGHT-GRAIN BINDING

1.   Cut crosswise strips of binding fabric the width called for in project instructions. Sew strips together end-to-end with a diagonal seam to achieve determined length.

2.   Matching wrong sides and raw edges, press strip in half lengthwise to complete binding.

ATTACHING BINDING WITH MITERED CORNERS

1.   Beginning with one end near center on bottom edge of quilt, lay binding around quilt to make sure that seams in binding will not end up at a corner. Adjust placement if necessary. Matching raw edges of binding to raw edge of quilt top, pin binding to right side of quilt along one edge.

2.   When you reach the first corner, mark ¹/₄" from corner of quilt top (**Fig. 24**).

3.   Beginning approximately 10" from end of binding and using a ¹/₄" seam allowance, sew binding to quilt, backstitching at beginning of stitching and at mark (**Fig. 25**). Lift needle out of fabric and clip thread.

4.   Fold binding as shown in **Figs. 26 and 27** and pin binding to adjacent side, matching raw edges. When you reach the next corner, mark ¹/₄" from edge of quilt top.

5.   Backstitching at edge of quilt top, sew pinned binding to quilt (**Fig. 28**); backstitch when you reach the next mark. Lift needle out of fabric and clip thread.

6.   Continue sewing binding to quilt, stopping approximately 10" from starting point (**Fig. 29**).

7.   Bring beginning and end of binding to center of opening and fold each end back, leaving a ¹/₄" space between folds (**Fig. 30**). Finger-press folds.

8. Unfold ends of binding and draw a line across wrong side in finger-pressed crease. Draw a line through the lengthwise pressed fold of binding at same spot to create a cross mark. With edge of ruler at marked cross, line up 45° angle marking on ruler with one long side of binding. Draw a diagonal line from edge to edge. Repeat on remaining end, making sure that the two lines are angled the same way (**Fig. 31**).

9. Matching right sides and diagonal lines, pin binding ends together at right angles (**Fig. 32**).

10. Machine stitch along diagonal line, removing pins as you stitch (**Fig. 33**).

11. Lay binding against quilt to double-check that it is correct length.

12. Trim binding ends, leaving $1/4$" seam allowance; press seam open. Stitch binding to quilt.

13. Trim backing and batting a scant $1/4$" larger than quilt top so that batting and backing will fill the binding when it is folded over to quilt backing.

14. On one edge of quilt, fold binding over to quilt backing and pin pressed edge in place, covering stitching line (**Fig. 34**). On adjacent side, fold binding over, forming a mitered corner (**Fig. 35**). Repeat to pin remainder of binding in place.

15. Blindstitch binding to backing, taking care not to stitch through to front of quilt.

Fig. 31

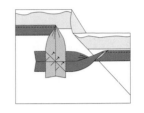

Fig. 32

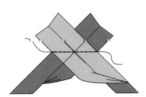

Fig. 33

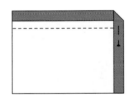

Fig. 34

Fig. 35

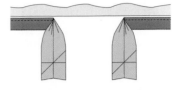

HAND STITCHES

Backstitch

Bring needle up at 1; go down at 2. Bring needle up at 3 and back down at 1 (**Fig. 36**). Continue working to make a continuous line of stitches.

Fig. 36

Blanket Stitch

Come up at 1. Go down at 2 , keeping thread below point of needle (**Fig. 37**). Continue working as shown in **Fig. 38**.

Fig. 37   **Fig. 38**

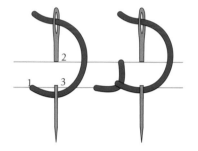

Blind Stitch

Come up at 1, go down at 2, and come up at 3 (**Fig. 39**). Length of stitches may be varied as desired.

Fig. 39

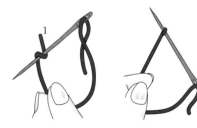

French Knot

Follow **Figs. 40 - 43** to complete French Knots. Come up at 1. Wrap thread once around needle and insert needle at 2, holding end of thread with non-stitching fingers. Tighten knot; then pull needle through, holding floss until it must be released.

Fig. 40   **Fig. 41**

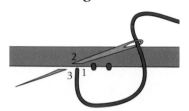

Fig. 42   **Fig. 43**

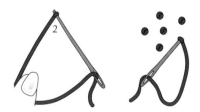

Running Stitch

The running stitch consists of a series of straight stitches with the stitch length equal to the space between stitches. Come up at 1, go down at 2, and come up at 3 (**Fig. 44**).

Satin Stitch

Come up at 1, go down at 2. Continue until area is filled (**Fig. 45**). Work stitches close together, but not overlapping.

Stem Stitch

Come up at 1. Keeping thread below the stitching line, go down at 2 and come up at 3. Go down at 4 and come up at 5 (**Fig. 46**).

Straight Stitch

Come up at 1 and go down at 2 (**Fig. 47**). Length of stitches may be varied as desired.

Fig. 44

Fig. 45

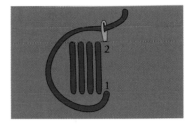

Fig. 46

Fig. 47

Metric Conversion Chart	
Inches x 2.54 = centimeters (cm)	Yards x .9144 = meters (m)
Inches x 25.4 = millimeters (mm)	Yards x 91.44 = centimeters (cm)
Inches x .0254 = meters (m)	Centimeters x .3937 = inches (")
	Meters x 1.0936 = yards (yd)

Standard Equivalents

1/8"	3.2 mm	0.32 cm	1/8 yard	11.43 cm	0.11 m
1/4"	6.35 mm	0.635 cm	1/4 yard	22.86 cm	0.23 m
3/8"	9.5 mm	0.95 cm	3/8 yard	34.29 cm	0.34 m
1/2"	12.7 mm	1.27 cm	1/2 yard	45.72 cm	0.46 m
5/8"	15.9 mm	1.59 cm	5/8 yard	57.15 cm	0.57 m
3/4"	19.1 mm	1.91 cm	3/4 yard	68.58 cm	0.69 m
7/8"	22.2 mm	2.22 cm	7/8 yard	80 cm	0.8 m
1"	25.4 mm	2.54 cm	1 yard	91.44 cm	0.91 m

Many thanks go to these ladies for their beautiful work.

Friendship Album was pieced by Valerie Schraml, quilted by Julie Schrader, bound by Glenda Taylor, and designed by Linda Tiano.

Production Team:
Technical Writer - Lisa Lancaster
Editorial Writer - Susan McManus Johnson
Graphic Artists – Stephanie Hamling and Andrea Hazelwood
Photography Stylist - Cassie Francioni

North Carolina Lily was pieced by Nelwyn Gray, quilted by Julie Schrader, bound by Diane Fischer, and designed by Frances Huddleston and Jean Lewis.